Patterns
A Collection of Poetry on Heartbreak and Possibility

by

Barrett Rosser

Table of Contents

2

3

Pattern: Heartbreak

Roll Of Thunder

took me by surprise
sunny eyes
an unexpected love.
charming, enchanting, confident, irresistible.

torrential tears flood a blurry vision trying to focus on reality.
consumed by jealousy and rage,
this heart won't beat
another thump if you leave.

please don't proceed to superseed my constant cries to
keep you
here with
me.

summers were unthinkable, winters too.

rolls of thunder...
ignite a fire fueled by passion
but
extinguished by love.
...hear my cry.

Love

must hurt since it never seems to stay.
maybe it's scared of my grasp.
petrified by scheming eyes.

once upon a time,
maybe you weren't ever mine.
sad out of the blue comes you but leaves, too.
too soon.
love's doomed.

Snip

wish it wasn't true
a soul devoured by love.
a heart so appeasing has become addicted to revealing
a side only God knew existed.

but the truth distorts its self
unbearably twisted in a tangled web of insecurities
suffocating passion in confusing contortions.

wild nights are set a blaze,
paths torched with deception
disguised with freak ass allabies.

green tears she cries...

drops of forest green
stain her cheeks
while he stains sheets
foreign to his passion.

Let Go

she cried inside
'cept no one knew.

salty stains trailed her cheeks.
a hurtful choice made every strong bone in her body meek.
but who's to say pain from the past leaves as time grows old?
it breathes and lives and cultivates and grabs a firm strong hold.

"let go" they chant sick themselves of her pouting face,
but she's not the one still holding on and
some lingering spirit she thought was gone
finds pleasure in her shame and disgrace.

an anonymous haunting reoccurring is daunting
and makes it close to impossible for her to see a real trace
of good in the choice that changed her life forever.

yet still her lovers fail to discover the pain she hides within.
disguised by pride and homicide
a lost soul inhabits her heart inside
and refuses to loosen its grip.

let go.

Emotional Bank Account: inthered

feelin' every which way
each and every day
tryina figure out who's who
who's true?

uneasy about the displeasing circumstances
I've been left in trances that defy laws of morals.
shit's been spoiled due to compromising situations
my heart's been misplaced in the wrong hands.

trying to love everyone but myself
ain't good for my health
and my wealth's been depleted
stolen by crooks that've looked to empty out my emotional bank account: I can't see straight.

hurt by too many withdrawals,
not enough deposits to keep me out the red.

my heart's bleeding
and I'm tired of loving everyone else but myself -
I'm done.

Another Poem...

I don't know you.
thought it'd be red- but you bleed blue.
deceived by what i believed was too good to be true
just too good to be you.

I live genuinely,
inspired by righteous warriors that triumph above handicaps.
but yet im handicapped by love.
paralyzed and stunted by lies.
brought me too close to my demise
and now it's no surprise that I'm numb.

in a love coma
couldn't get any colder.
terrorized by a sneak, a snake
now the great debate isn't between me and you
but between a broken heart needin' healin' from a forgivin' lover
and the constant yearnin' to love someone that really isn't even you.

EGhOst

you're not here
but still everywhere i wish you weren't.
more in my life now that you aren't.

you rumble the closet
where you used to hide
and all these lonesome mornings
you've come back to reside
in my mind
taunting me
with hauntings of a love that
can
never
be
because your ego won't let
you
love
me.

Unpredictable

you're an avid believer in unpredictability.
you live and breathe by it.

so often that the odds are almost always stacked against us,
so when you swear you love me,
I can't forget to call your bluff.

nothing's ever guaranteed
that must be why you contemplate to proceed
with us.

but just as sure as there's a god in the heavens
just as sure as six always comes before seven-
no sourcerer would predict,
no gambler would bet,
no drunk would drink
against my love.

it shapes the dynamics of my heartbeat
sets a pace for the blood runnin' through my veins
slips and slides down your manhood when I come to a place
where only truth thrives.

how long will it take for you to believe that what you feel is real?

Sanctuary

running.
running out of trust .
running into a dead end
where dead friends, dead mothers, dead lovers
only child: no sisters, no brothers, where
the messenger cultivates more sin than the message, where
the prayer can't undo the damage of a mistreated blessing, where
the air scares itself up and out of the lungs
of a broken body, exhausted- no longer in search of answers or anybody.

dead friends, dead mothers, dead fathers, dead lovers,
only child- no sisters, no brothers.
eyes tightly shut, hands grasped around her throat
in over her head, no light, the least bit of remote
control to rewind time, change the minds of those that find comfort in lies.
victimized, blamed, & ashamed-
i find comfort in sighs
just b r e a t h e- the air's my only friend
all else has failed & now
my sanctuary is this dead end.

Fades are Inevitable

wish upon your stars.
love long love hard.
cry for every little reason.
cause when it starts to fade...

when loves deep waters resign to an even deeper grave,
everything that kept you there
all those times you swore you'd make him swear to never leave,
every step taken to correct the stress
each & every text and all that "he said she said" mess
doesn't even matter
cause
you've faded.

but remember what it was.
smile at the thought of what you know you & him will never be.

reminisce of the bliss that sent butterflies a float
from your toes to your nose at the very taste of each and every kiss.

laugh at the next lifetime
and know there will never be a right time for you & him to be one.
no regrets, no regrets, just love undone.
love that let you live in its rapture for a season
but realize there's a reason that you've
faded.

fading was inevitable with us.

Nuffin but a Fuckin

"i love you.
no really i do.
what? don't you believe in loving two?
yo for real, i swear my love is true!-
whatchu mean you never knew?
..."

so she checks his eyes for a superficial glaze
replays his words, thinkin maybe its a phase
but then he pulls her closer
softly rubs her place
and she screams inside while staring in his face.

"I love you" strikes her like fire
every single syllable fuels her flammable desire.

funny what 48 hours will do...

"you know i don't even really remember what i said,
Maybe, possibly, i was thinkin with the wrong head?
You're cool and all but this thing we got needs to be put to bed-
maaan stop being so emotional, the subject is dead!"

Well so was her spirit
he carried it to the heavens
and then dragged it back to sorrow
she hated those words he spoke three days before tomorrow

he didn't love two
just his baby mava &
his otha part-time lova's lovin
that was never really nuffin
she was never really nuffin
nuffin but a fuckin.

3 one-syllable words

more than any sound on earth
i'd rather hear your lips give birth to
3
one
syllabled
words.
three words, when heard
cling to my ears
slide down my neck,
take a quick breath 'round my breasts
and without rest, rise & set
every single vowel & consonant
in my chest.

summer could sing,
stars could brilliantly ring,
but there would only be 1 choice,
all i'd wanna hear is your voice.

your voice echoing in my being,
the sound of longevity,
for all eternity,

I love you.

Reject

amongst the jagged edges of his piercing dialect
you can still detect the love his mind insists he must reject.

and although one can maybe trail his Legendary stains
harmonizing with the walls of another woman's pains,
there's no mistake of where he wants to be:
in the arms of a shrew whose taming'll set him free.

the stench of a weathered romance seeps from his skin
but the aroma of his roomate, Corona, keeps the love smell thin-
as his favorite foreign vaginas engulf him in sin
some epiphany is resurrected from his tainted soul within...
she is where he wants to be.

so no matter how many good fucks his heart has regretfully cursed and kept
even all of those part-time pussy's can successfully bet
that amongst the jagged edges of his piercing dialect
you can still detect the love his mind insists he must reject.

in this life and the next.

I Think I'm Crazy

nothing is nothing at all.
i feel like curling up into a ball.
a ball of nothing at all.
nothing will break this fall.
i'm falling with nothing at all to break this fall.
the people that call know nothing at all.
they call with words that haul my existence into hell's air.
my soul is empty and bare, nothing is there.
nothing at all.*

*see title

Scream

screams aren't loud enough &
eardrums run from words undone.
patience is the enemy.

daydream with me in mind.
these screams can't break your trance.
daydream with me in mind.
receive these gentle hints of a sweet romance.

believe in who u have to be
but hear me screaming,
please.

Miserable

somewhere on common ground, a miserable love was found.

the sweet stink of pink roses
the sweet ink that writes poems is
accountable for this mess.

in misery im dying to address
a love undone by one
who's fun is limitless.

sweet links of soft kisses
miserable love only wishes
that misery haunted two.

you see shallow reasons
and when spring seems like all four seasons
you rush to break from gravity's hold...
spirits you conquer, capturing hearts and souls.

selfish thoughts provoke you not to stay around
you're self professed and proudly profound
sweet cries from eyes echo a melancholy sound...
and somewhere on common ground
a miserable love is found.

Being

just being
sometimes is a challenge.

being, living, breathing, steady
reminiscing of the loves that passed me by.

even being is hard when i close my eyes and try to
forget the faces that took my heart places
where the sun don't shine.

being me in a world of no promises
makes me feel like life lies
and although i try
I never quite measure up.

I need just one gentle touch
that'll make me feel like being is
really worth it.
worth being.

Pinch me

I'm lost.
are things parallel
or perpendicular
in this more than peculiar
predicament I've found myself in?

pinch me.

im sinking in the thought
of finally staying afloat
in waters that bare me no harm.

cast me ashore on the
pleasant paradise of a place
called your heart.

let confusion die and clouds disappear
from the sky in the essence of
the light from your presence
that shines on this island of
complete oneness and unity
that i dream for me and you.

Help – Love

"help."

help is what she said when she awoke from her nap...
it was right around the time when the sun and the earth closed its gap.

as the blue sky of the day shows her yellow warmth of what is to be night,
her emotions run wildy in anticipation of some sign that she'll be alright
help is what she said just as the tears started clouding her sight.

for years though, there had been something wrong with her vision
never focusing on what ought to be valued,
only the sickening ill's of love that wrote her no prescription.

constantly hurting her - love.
always deserting her - love.
using and abusing her - love.
misleading not treating her - love.
name calling controlling her - love.
bounded to sadness - love.
confined to madness - love.
stressed and depressed - love.
never at best - love.

"help."

help is what I say as the darkness creeps into the room.
alone and frustrated, all this melancholy energy I consume.
coughing, and sneezing, aching in pain
help me someone... break these hurtful chains,
i'm trying so hard not to go insane,
alive is all I am trying to remain
can someone please explain why it wont refrain from causing me so much pain -

LOVE.

Pattern: Possibility

Happy

they sedate me temporarily
and momentarily i feel extraordinarily happy.
no more pain, so the disdain my life attains remains secluded
and for a moment I'm sane.

this isnt the best solution
but this temporary pain killer is a thriller
and for once i fill her shoes
the woman i aspire to be.

and all the debris that resonates
from the harsh quarrels and stupid debates
don't matter because I'm sedated.

they make me happy!

until the high dies down
smile turn to frown
and everyone is around
ready to surround me and drown me
deep in my imperfections.

ready to hurt and divert
every ounce of faith into waste
and bring me back to reality
back to the real bee
whose mentality fights with the morality
that keeps me teetering in between everything good and bad.

Cane and Abel live to disable me
so sick of functioning improperly,
so I take them to sedate me temporarily
and momentarily i feel extraordinarily happy.

Touch

just remembering your touch
makes me yearn to find the words beautiful enough to write this poem.

what was black faded gray
and it took me way into a dreamland with ice cream and raindrops dipped in sun.
a remarkable place it was to be a victim of your touch.

I can remember when I'd surrender to your kiss...
your kiss, oh your kiss was bliss.
bliss that was equivalent to tears of joy,
the birth of a new baby boy,
something just remarkable i have never felt
i love to remember how you felt your skin topping mine.

memories surface making it hard for me to forget
not at all do i regret those encounters our senses made.

or how our souls collided,
my burdens were lightened
and still at the slightest sounds, the simplest words, the easiest song
those memories linger in the front of my mind to remind me how much I loved your touch.

I loved you so much.

Smoker's Delight

an indescribable high suddenly finds a way to translate:

my lips smile- times two.
ignites a fire so hot it's blue.
rights all wrongs,
a never-ending long love song
like "lets get it on" & "on & on"
marvin & badu bleed through
this high, suffocating its smokers up on cloud 9.

Take another pull, keep with the love smokin' us
keep the love smokin' us
keep the love choking thrusts
keep the drug soaking up
every ounce of doubt-
even sends smoke signals from NY to down south.

Not to NC
but to a newly restored heart
infused with a tainted drug my system needs to survive,
I need my fix to stay alive, while

Intoxicating pulls keep me opposite of dry-
keeps passing the smoke & im incredibly high
he got me so love-struck i'm looking down at the sky-

smoker's delight.

Heartsquared

your heart is in mine
two sets of beats separate time.
if one skips a thump, the other triumphs & relinquishes its strength
your heart is in mine & i'm finally content.

never knew there was room for 2
until i woke up alone &
felt your muscle at home
home is where your heart is.
there's no doubt that we'll finish what we've started
taking flight we have now departed,
from the land of the broken hearted
pleasantly surprised by all the baggage we've disregarded.

your heart is in mine
our lives are entwined,
the pain has declined,
so we're twice as inclined,
2 find no greater love than that of
the sacred place in my chest.

your heart is in mine...
and sorrow has finally been put to rest.

Sistas and Brothas

if it ain't one thing
it's another.
lonely sistahs, lonely brothas
always seek another's lover.

frustration lies in the eyes
of a woman scorned.
just her luck
she feels torn.

however, Karma speculates the hate
only the devil could create
and seeks to negate
the wrongdoings of the lonely hearted.

irony at its best must
test the bond of love only once she has departed.
must be easy to try'n spark a flame
in the deserted fields of your soul.

dare not tempt my other half in spite of your rage
let love be your goal.

Keepinupwiththe…

time collides
souls intertwine
and finally
my mind's in sync with my heart.
they try to keep up
but have no luck
cause the Jones knows there's more to life than greed.
empty temptation may seem like a need
to hos that hold no bars.
is this love that I'm feelin?
cause his love drug's revealin'
to heal much more than minor scars.

Unwritten Words

unwritten words have filled blank pages of my conscience.
seems like the messages just couldn't develop
stunted by years of anguish,
unwritten words were left unsaid
my poetry was dead...
right along with me.

but somehow a renaissance has commenced.
stories untold unlock and unfold the solitary grave of my heart,
so now, finally, these unwritten words can depart
since love has gotten a fresh breath... a new start.

Area

situations negate the meaningful good circumferenced in the area of one's being.
odd ball out shines bright a light that real often recognize seeing.
opposing forces roll out a blinding rationale
but what is straight inevitably prevails
until a crooked sight illuminates a glow casting a shadow over cruel intentions-
an unfamiliar face foreign to anything true.
now what it sees isn't you.

still empathy resides in a heart so big
amongst others who can get a taste.
so sweet a big heart
that crooked sight dare not let it go to waste.
now let's retrace the time and place
when moments transcend the most recent debates.
regret not the past
love the hate you can't reciprocate
the lies that came too late
the mistakes that made you great
the frauds and their mates
the temporary joy that filled your plate

still so good to be alive
to breathe through strangulation
others wished they could survive.

keep growing rose
keep progressing through the dirt
for all you ever were, are, will be
and the entire area of your worth.

The Show

now, rather than negate the hate
she must live by the code they hold.
see what matters is the audience... right?
so she's caste in a part that reciprocates
ambiguous oxymorons set by people who salute society.

but it doesn't even matter.

walk that walk, talk that talk,
do that dance, clean those pans!

god forbid you leave ya mark or don't.
either way that pretty picture will be a
pimp's portrait laid up in filth
too lost to leave the dark.

enslaved by the part she must play,
she's a puppet in immoral hierarchies
stuck in castes that are causally common to an obliging audience.

so here's ya chance, girl.
ride that wave, or do that dance.
no matter which road you take
make every move a move you make
not for them but
for His sake.

see maybe what they don't know
is that it's really His show.

so be a puppet if you want....

Chocolate

chocolate resonates gracefully upon his skin
I wish I could taste it.

his tender lips i'd send to sin
if i could only taste them.

and when we're alone in a room of crowded people
a foreign spotlight hits my spot right

as he bats his eyes in my direction,
most times I'm the one he's speaking to
but my conscience makes that quick correction.

often i appease my imagination
with a subtle unnoticed gravitation
towards his sinful skin

i'd love the taste of chocolate
i'd love to be with him.

Really Love

everything perfect is possible with you.
skies rise high above aggravated times
and rhymes flow like wine when we celebrate.

finally a love that lasts longer than a hot fuck or a cheap date.
confusion takes a back seat to love that grasps longevity.
& at times i find myself panting and breathing heavily
because i am steadily

adjusting to the fact that
you really do love me.

Love Cup

My voice shakes, and my body shivers like I'm cold.
Think this is my ancestors, shaking shit up.
They pushed honesty from my throat chakra as I painted on the canvas of my life.
The little one is confused, but I'm not.
Said I'm ready to love, but I am love, I am it. Pouring into my cup first, my frame shakes reverberating through hairline fractures.
Let me seal it up.
Love is my glue.
I'm the glue.
Calmly pouring.
Gently sipping.
Steady hands, head, breath and heart.
I love you.

Delectable

Wherever you are, whoever you are,
I'm living the life of my dreams,
and I'm excited to meet you living out yours.

I'm deep in my vision, creating. I know you are, too.
And when I close my eyes and breathe,
I be the love, fulfillment, adventure and possibilities our union will source.

Loving myself is so delicious
and for you to be a witness will be delectable,
you'll be delectable, too.

I love you.

Tired
featuring Toni Cobb

Lord knows I get tired of being tired.
Feels like I'm dragging my heart and soul.
How much mental and physical anguish can my body hold?

Or are my heart and soul dragging me?
Topped off with anger, my body's filled to the brim.
Seeking solace in the empty hands of others has been grim.

Lord knows I get tired of being tired.
So I'll rest easy in my integrity.
Lean in and listen to my guides attentively.
Give myself permission to find agency in grief,
move to acceptance from shock and disbelief.

And when I've finally managed to rehabilitate my heart,
I'll never forget my tired and weary start.

To My Eternal Love

Your love has always moved like water.

Infinite and vast,
calming and crashing,
consistent and thirst quenching,
healing, whole and engulfing;
a lifetime of water, a lifetime of you...
never drowning always afloat
the waves, they kept us, and will keep us, still.

Water moves like spirit and time,
All fluid, like my love for you.

Like the rain beating the pavement outside my window
like the sweet and hot summer dew
like the water that's always filled my cup
like tears that meet the air...
It's all delicious.

Our love is like water, fluid, like spirit and time.
In every form, in every fashion,
our love will flow forever even in goodbye.

I will love you always,
Toni